Modest Petrovich
Moussorgsky

Pictures at an Exhibition
and Other Works
for Piano

Edited by Pavel Lamm
for the Complete Works Edition

DOVER PUBLICATIONS, INC., New York

This Dover edition, first published in 1990, is a republication of Vol. VIII: *Pièces
pour Piano/Fortepiannïe sočineniĭa* from M. Moussorgsky, *Oeuvres Complètes/Polnoe
sobranie sočineniĭ*, originally published by Editions de Musique de l'URSS/Gosu-
darstvennoe Muzïkal'noe Izdatel'stvo, Moscow and Leningrad, 1939. The editor's
foreword has been omitted. The footnotes, stage directions and composer's datings
in Russian and French have been translated into English.
We are grateful to Dr. Vladimir Leyetchkiss for the loan of the score for
reproduction.

Manufactured in the United States of America
Dover Publications, Inc., 31 East 2nd Street, Mineola, N.Y. 11501

Library of Congress Cataloging-in-Publication Data

Mussorgsky, Modest Petrovich, 1839–1881.
    Pictures at an exhibition and other works for piano.

    Reprint. Originally published: Moscow : Editions de musique de l'URSS, 1939.
(Œuvres complètes / M. Moussorgsky ; v. 8).
    Contents: Souvenir d'enfance—Scherzo in C-sharp minor : 1st version —[etc.]—
Hopak of the young Ukrainians : 2nd version.
    1. Piano music. 2. Suites (Piano). 3. Sonatas (Piano, 4 hands). I. Lamm,
P. (Pavel), 1882—1951. II. Title.
M22.M975P54   1990   90-752263
ISBN 0-486-26515-3

CONTENTS

Pictures at an Exhibition and Other Works for Piano

Childhood Memory

[Воспоминание детства]   Souvenir d' enfance

¹The key signature has been changed by the editor.

16 October 1857. M. Moussorgsky.

———————————

[1]The key signature has been changed by the editor.

Scherzo in C-sharp Minor

1st version

Скерцо

[Первое изложение]

[Scherzo]

[Première version]

Allegro assai

Allegro assai (Tempo I)

25 November 1858. Modest Moussorgsky

Scherzo in C-sharp Minor

2nd version

Скерцо

[Второе изложение]

[Scherzo]

[Deuxième version]

Allegro non troppo

p staccato

16   *Scherzo: 2nd version*

Allegro non troppo (Tempo I)

St. Petersburg. Modest Moussorgsky.

Ein Kinder-Scherzo (A Child's Scherzo)

1st version

Детские игры-уголки

(скерцо)

[Первое изложение]

[„ EIN KINDERSCHERZ"]

[Jeux d'enfants-les quatre coins]

(scherzo)

[Premiere version]

¹In autograph no. 420 the right hand is written as:

[1] In autograph no. 420 this passage is written thus:

[1] ¹In autograph no. 420 the left hand in the succeeding five measures is written staccato.

²In autograph no. 420 the succeeding 16 measures are written thus:

[1]In autograph no. 420 the right hand is written thus:

[2]In autograph no. 420 the left hand in the succeeding five measures is written staccato.

[3]See note 2, p. 25.

[1]In autograph no. 420 the left hand is written thus:

[1]In autograph no. 420 the succeeding 34 measures are missing. [Footnote reference missing in the original Lamm edition.]

Ein Kinder-Scherzo: 1st version 29

¹In autograph no. 420 this passage is written thus:

²In autograph no. 420 the left hand is written thus:

²In autograph no. 420 the right hand is written thus:

[1] In autograph no. 420 the bass part is written thus:

[2] In autograph no. 420 the bass part is written thus:

[3] In autograph no. 420 the bass part is written thus:

[4] In autograph no. 420 this passage is written thus:

[1] In autograph no. 420 the succeeding 16 measures are written thus:

26 September 1859

¹In autograph no. 420 this passage is written thus:

Ein Kinder-Scherzo (A Child's Scherzo)

2nd version

Детские игры- уголки   [Jeux d'enfants-les quatre coins]

„EIN KINDERSCHERZ"

[Второе изложение]   [Deuxième version]

Schnell [Скоро]

40   *Ein Kinder-Scherzo: 2nd version*

44   *Ein Kinder-Scherzo: 2nd version*

28 May 1860.

Passionate Impromptu (Recollection of Beltov and Lyuba)
1st version

Impromptu [passionné]
[Воспоминание о Бельтове и Любе]
[Первое изложение]

[Impromptu passionné]
[Souvenir de Beltov et Liouba]
[Première version]

[1]It is to this passage that autograph no. 7 pertains; we quote it in its entirety:

*End of autograph no. 7.

St. Petersburg. Modest Moussorgsky

Passionate Impromptu (Recollection of Beltov and Lyuba)
2nd version

Impromptu passionné
(Воспоминание о Бельтове и Любе)

[Второе изложение]

[Impromptu passionné]
[Souvenir de Beltov et Liouba]

[Deuxième version]

1 October 1859. Modest Moussorgsky.

Sonata in C Major
for piano four hands

Соната

[Sonate]

[для фортепиано в 4 руки]

[Pour piano à 4 mains]

I

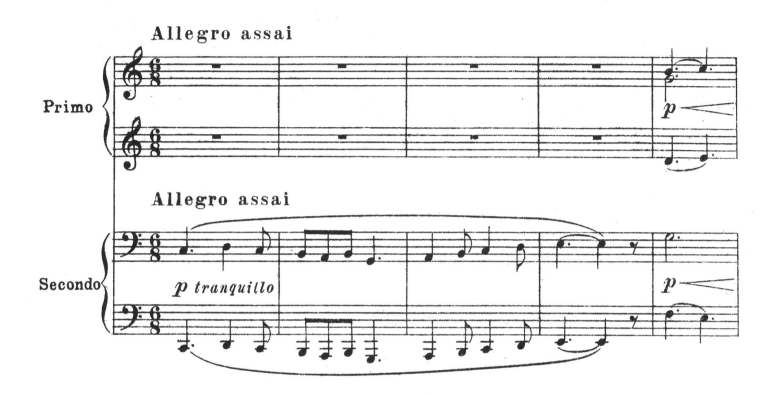

¹Note in red pencil on autograph no. 404: "Must be repeated once again from the beginning."

¹At this point in autograph no. 404 the following two measures are crossed out in ink:

[1]At this point in autograph no. 404 the following 23 measures are crossed out in ink:

[1] In autograph no. 404 the parallel fifths in the upper part are marked thus in red pencil:

¹In autograph no. 404 the bass part bears the inscription: "Bitte recht stark, liebe Trombone" [Good and strong, please, dear trombones].

poco più accelerando

¹In autograph no. 404 the part of the pianist who sits on the right bears the inscription "s'il vous plaît."

Sonata for piano four hands   65

[1]At this point in autograph no. 404 the following two measures are crossed out in ink:

8 December 1860. Modest Moussorgsky.

II

SCHERZO [1]

[1]There exists an earlier version of this Scherzo (1858) for piano two hands, transposed to C-sharp minor—see page 7; also a variant of the Scherzo (of unknown date), likewise for piano two hands and in C-sharp minor—see page 14.

Allegro non troppo (Tempo I)

Allegro non troppo (Tempo I)

[1]In autograph no. 404 the reprise is not written out.

From Memories of Childhood

Няня и я   1. Nurse and I   [Niania et moi]

„Из воспоминаний детства" № 1   [„Souvenirs d'enfance" № 1]

Довольно медленно [Moderato assai]

simile

22 April 1865. St. Petersburg. M. Moussorgsky.

From Memories of Childhood   89

2. First Punishment (Nurse Shuts Me in a Dark Room)

Первое наказание

[Première punition]

„Из воспоминаний детства" № 2
(Няня запирает меня в темную комнату)

[„Souvenirs d'enfance" № 2]
[Niania m'enferme dans le cabinet noir]

Быстро [Vivo]

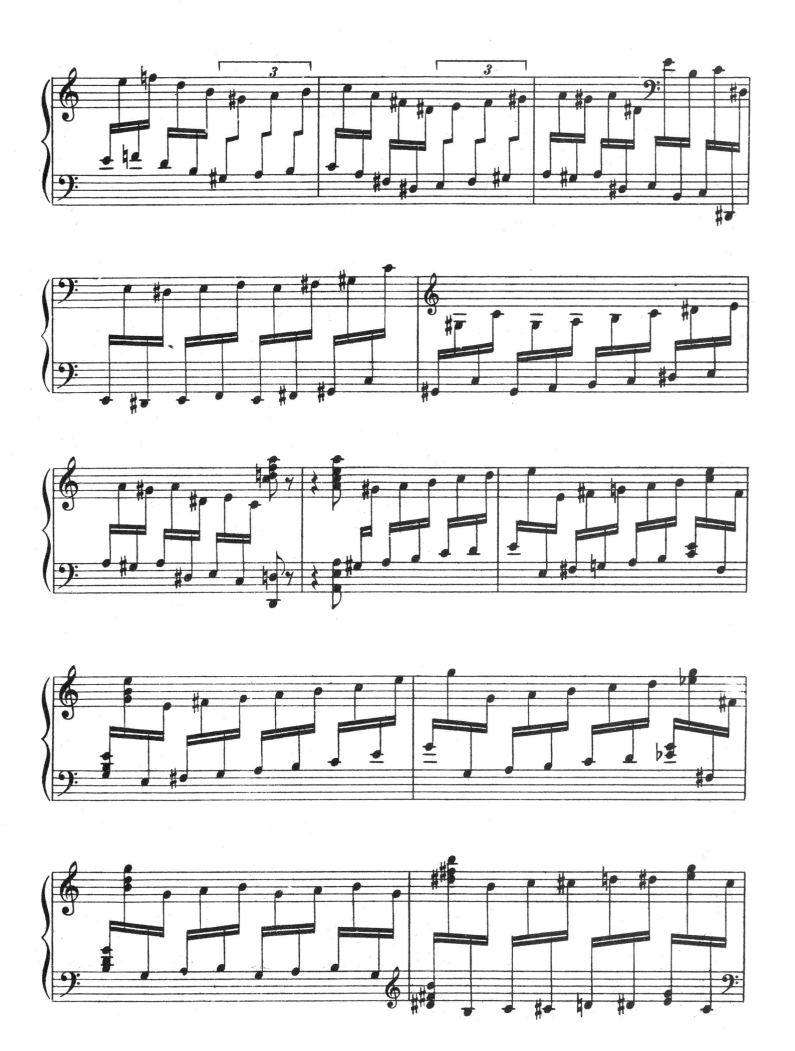

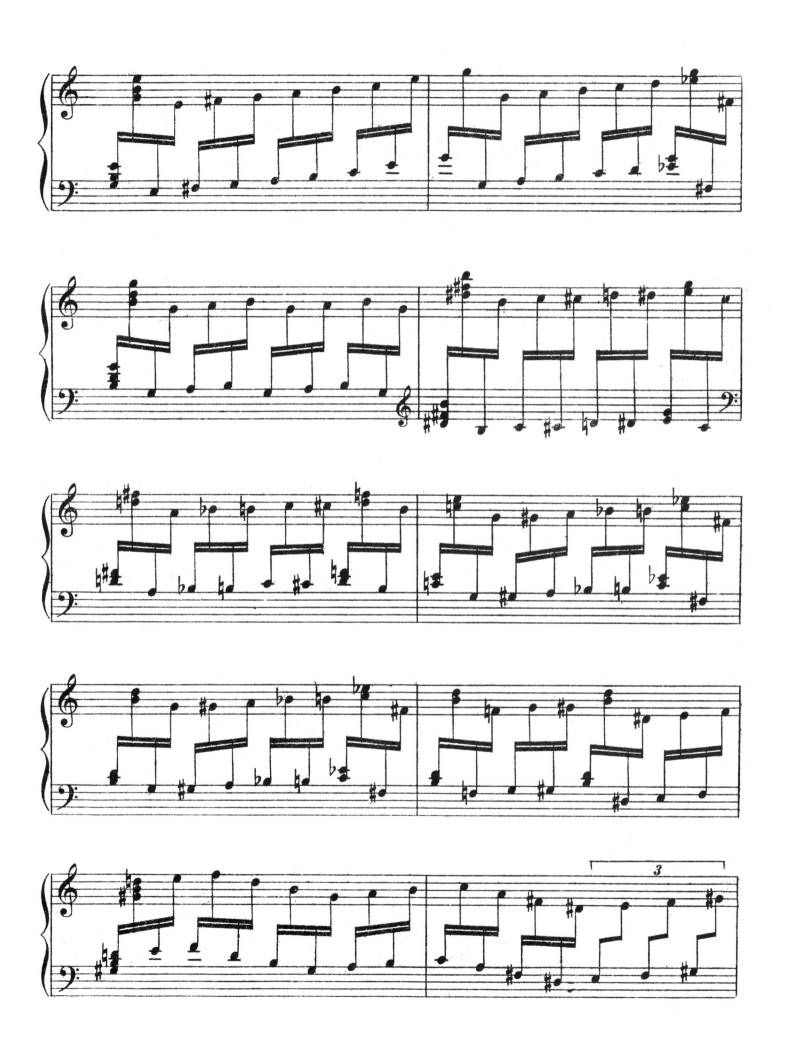

*Here autographs nos. 12 and 304 break off; the ending, not very successful stylistically, is taken from the edition by V. G. Karatïgin.

Reverie

Дума

[Rêverie]

Theme by V. Loginov

Довольно медленно [Assez lent]

rit.   a tempo

22 July 1865. Modest Moussorgsky.

The Capricious One

[Шалунья]   La capricieuse

Theme by Count L. Geïden

Capriccio

Постепенно замедляя
[Rallentando poco a poco]

26 July 1865. Modest Moussorgsky.

La capricieuse   103

Symphonic Intermezzo in the Classic Manner

1st version

Intermezzo symphonique

IN MODO CLASSICO

[Первое изложение для фортепиано]   [Première version pour piano]

Grave, pesante

Intermezzo symphonique in modo classico: 1st version

Symphonic Intermezzo in the Classic Manner

Transcription of orchestral version

Интермеццо
(IN MODO CLASSICO)

[Второе изложение]
для оркестра

Фортепианное переложение в 2 руки сочинителя

[Intermezzo]
[IN MODO CLASSICO]

[Deuxième version]
[pour orchestre]

[Transcription pour piano à deux mains par l'auteur]

Строго. [Grave. Pesante]

―――――――――――――――――――――

*The rehearsal numbers have been added by the editor to correspond to the orchestral score.

Intermezzo symphonique in modo classico: orchestral version

July 1867. Minkino Farm. M. Moussorgsky.

Pictures at an Exhibition
Картинки с выставки.   Tableaux d'une exposition.

Promenade

[Прогулка.]   Promenade.

Allegro giusto, nel modo russico, senza allegrezza, ma poco sostenuto.

attacca

1. Gnome

[Гном.]   № 1.   Gnomus.

[1]This measure as written by Moussorgsky differs from the two musically analogous measures marked on the staves above with asterisks (C♮ in place of B♭).

[1] At this point in the autograph there is a measure crossed out in ink by the composer:

[2] At this point in the autograph there is a measure crossed out in ink by the composer:

[3] At this point in the autograph there is a whole line (8 measures) crossed out in ink by the composer:

[4] This measure as written by Moussorgsky differs from the musically analogous measure marked in the staff above with an asterisk (E♭ in place of D).

Moderato commodo assai e con delicatezza.

2. The Old Castle

[Старый замокъ.]   №2   Il vecchio castello.

Andantino molto cantabile e con dolore.

Moderato non tanto, pesamente.

---
¹The key signature was provided by the editor.

3. Tuileries (Children's Quarrel After Playing)

[Тюльерийский сад] № 3. Tuileries

[Ссора детей после игры] (Dispute d' enfants après jeux.)

Allegretto non troppo, capriccioso

4. Oxen (The Oxcart)

[Быдло.]   №4.   Bydlo.

Sempre moderato, pesante.

[1]The key signature was provided by the editor.

5. Ballet of the Unhatched Chicks

Балет не вылупившихся птенцов. №5. [Ballet des poussins dans leurs coques.]

¹The title is written in pencil in the autograph in Moussorgsky's hand.

Pictures at an Exhibition 139

Da Capo il Scherzino, senza Trio, e poi Coda

Coda

attacca

¹The upper part is written in the autograph in the following manner: etc., which, in keeping with Moussorgsky's habitual notational practice, signifies trills that begin on the main note.

6. Two Jews, One Rich and the Other Poor (Samuel Goldenberg and Schmuyle)

[Два еврея,
богатый и бедный.]   № 6.   [Deux juifs l'un
riche et l'autre pauvre.]

[Прогулка.]   Promenade.

Allegro giusto, nel modo russico, poco sostenuto.

*At this point in the autograph there appears the following (French-language) text, struck out in ink by Moussorgsky:

No. 7. Limoges; the market.

The big news: Mr. Pimpant [smart dresser] of Panta Pantaleon has just found his cow Runaway. "Yes, ma'am, it was yesterday." "No, ma'am, it was the day before." "I assure you, ma'am, the animal was roaming in the neighborhood." "Just the opposite, ma'am, the animal was not roaming at all." Etc.

*Before this piece in the autograph there appears the following (French) text, struck out in ink by Moussorgsky:

The big news: Mr. Puissangeout has just found his cow Runaway. But the good ladies of Limoges are not quite in agreement on the matter, because Mrs. Remboursac has appropriated a lovely porcelain denture while Mr. Panta-Pantaleon still has his annoying peony-red nose.

Meno mosso, sempre capriccioso.

poco accelerando

attacca

8. Catacombs. Roman Sepulchre

[Катакомбы.]   № 8.   Catacombae.

[Римская гробница.]   Sepulcrum romanum.

*[С мертвыми на мертвом языке.   Con mortuis in lingua mortua.]

Andante non troppo, con lamento

*Before this section in the autograph there appears the following note by Moussorgsky (in Russian):

N.B.: Latin text: with the dead in a dead language. A Latin text would be suitable: the creative spirit of the late Hartmann [Gartman] leads me to skulls, summons me to them, the skulls have quietly lit up.

Избушка на курьих ножках.　№9.　[La cabane sur des pattes de poule.]

(Баба-Яга)　　　　　　　　　　　[Baba-Jaga]

Allegro con brio, feroce.

*The following passage was written by Moussorgsky originally, then struck out in ink and covered with a glued strip:

Allegro molto.

10. The Great Gate (in the Capital, Kiev)

Богатырские ворота.   № 10.   [La grande porte.]

В стольном городе во Киеве.   [Dans la capitale de Kiev.]

Allegro alla breve. Maestoso. Con grandezza.

[1]There follow in the autograph two measures struck out in ink by the composer:

[1]From this measure on, this passage was originally written differently by Moussorgsky, but later it was covered by a glued strip, without being crossed out:

Meno mosso, sempre maestoso.

22 June 1874, Petrograd. M. Moussorgsky.

On the Southern Shore of the Crimea (Gurzuf)

На южном берегу Крыма

Гхурзуф у Аю-дага (Юрзуф)

Из путевых заметок

[En Crimée]

[Ghourzouff. Notes de voyage]

Moderato scherzando. Leggiero

Meditation
Album Leaf

[Раздумье]   Méditation

[Листок из альбома]   Feuillet d'album

[1]In autograph no. 284 the bass part was originally written thus:

a tempo

poco ritard.   più ritard.

A tempo; cantabile

poco rit.

a tempo

poco rit.

---

[1]In autograph no. 284 the bass part was originally written thus:

Largamente.

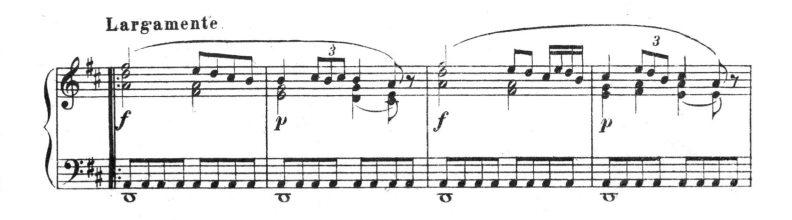

ritard.   Poco meno mosso

Più meno mosso

ritard.

M. Moussorgsky.

A Tear
(Quasi fantasia)

[Слеза]　　　　　　　Une larme

M. Moussorgsky.

The Seamstress
Scherzino

Швея
[СКЕРЦИНО]

[La couturière]
SCHERZINO

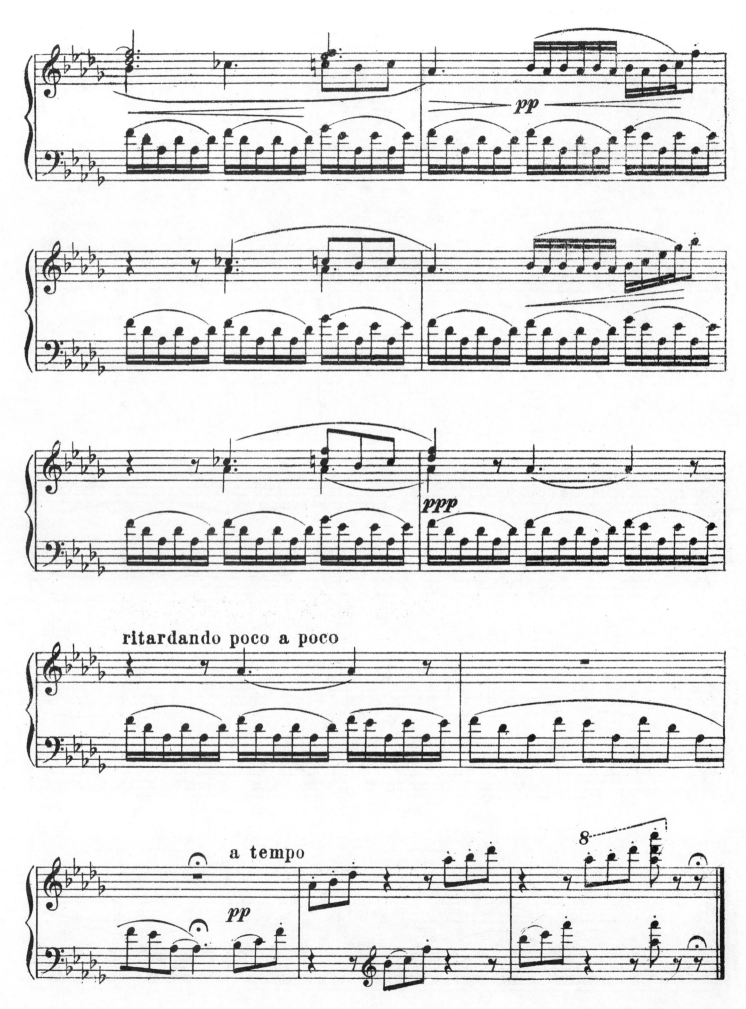

M. Moussorgsky.

Near the Southern Shore of the Crimea: Capriccio (Baidari)

Близ южного берега Крыма

[En Crimée]

БАЙДАРКИ КАПРИЧИО

[CAPRICCIO]

Гхурсуф у Аю-Дага (Юрзуф)

[Ghourzouff. Notes de voyage.]

Из путевых заметок

Near the Southern Shore of the Crimea

January 1880. M. Moussorgsky.

Near the Southern Shore of the Crimea 189

In the Village

В деревне

[Au village]

Fair Scene
from *The Fair at Sorochintsy*

Ярмарочная сцена

из оперы

„Сорочинская ярмарка"

Транскрипция для фортепиано автора

[Scène de foire]

[de l'opèra]

[„La foire de Sorotchintsy"]

[Transcription pour piano par l'auteur]

Moderato marziale

Group of young Ukrainians

Gypsies, who earn their living heaven knows how

Young Ukrainians

Same Gypsies

ritard.

Poco meno mosso. *Delicatissimo*

Parassia, accompanied by her father, feasts her eyes on the ribbons and caps.

Moderato, scherzando

Group of young girls

Giocoso

Young Ukrainians

Same young girls

Andantino con moto

Gypsy directing the comedy. Quasi deus ex machina.

allargando

Gypsy (to use the usual expression) "taking someone in"

M. Moussorgsky.

Hopak of the Merry Young Ukrainians

from *The Fair at Sorochintsy:* 1st version

Гопак веселых паробков

из оперы

„Сорочинская ярмарка"

[Первое изложение]

Транскрипция для фортепиано автора

[Hopak[1] de jeunes ukrainiens gaillards]

[fragment de l'opera]

[„La foire de Sorotchintsy"]

[Première version]

[Transcription pour piano par l'auteur]

---

[1]Ukrainian national dance.
[2]At this measure, autograph no. 272 begins.

¹At this measure, autograph no. 272 breaks off.

Hopak of the Young Ukrainians
from *The Fair at Sorochintsy:* 2nd version

Гопак веселых па̀робков

из оперы

„Сорочинская ярмарка"

[Второе изложение]

Транскрипция для фортепиано автора

[Hopak[1] de jeunes ukrainiens]

[fragment de l'opéra]

[La foire de Sorotchintsy]

[Deuxième version]

[Transcription pour piano par l'auteur]

[1]Hopak—Ukrainian national dance.
[2]After autograph no. 274.

¹Here autograph no. 274 breaks off and autograph no. 276 begins.

¹Here autograph no. 276 breaks off and autograph no. 277 begins.

Dover Piano and Keyboard Editions

SHORTER WORKS FOR PIANOFORTE SOLO, Franz Schubert. All piano music except Sonatas, Dances, and a few unfinished pieces. Contains Wanderer, Impromptus, Moments Musicals, Variations, Scherzi, etc. Breitkopf and Härtel edition. 199pp. 9⅜ × 12¼. 22648-4 Pa. **$12.95**

WALTZES AND SCHERZOS, Frédéric Chopin. All of the Scherzos and nearly all (20) of the Waltzes from the authoritative Mikuli edition. Editorial commentary. 160pp. 9 × 12. 24316-8 Pa. **$9.95**

COMPLETE PRELUDES AND ETUDES FOR SOLO PIANO, Frédéric Chopin. All 25 Preludes, all 27 Etudes by greatest composer of piano music. Authoritative Mikuli edition. 192pp. 9 × 12. 24052-5 Pa. **$8.95**

COMPLETE BALLADES, IMPROMPTUS AND SONATAS, Frédéric Chopin. The four Ballades, four Impromptus and three Sonatas. Authoritative Mikuli edition. 192pp. 9 × 12. 24164-5 Pa. **$10.95**

NOCTURNES AND POLONAISES, Frédéric Chopin. 20 *Nocturnes* and 11 *Polonaises* reproduced from the authoritative Mikuli edition for pianists, students, and musicologists. Commentary. 224pp. 9 × 12. 24564-0 Pa. **$10.95**

COMPLETE MAZURKAS, Frédéric Chopin. 51 best-loved compositions, reproduced directly from the authoritative Kistner edition edited by Carl Mikuli. 160pp. 9 × 12. 25548-4 Pa. **$8.95**

FANTASY IN F MINOR, BARCAROLLE, BERCEUSE AND OTHER WORKS FOR SOLO PIANO, Frédéric Chopin. 15 works, including one of the greatest of the Romantic period, the Fantasy in F Minor, Op. 49, reprinted from the authoritative German edition prepared by Chopin's student, Carl Mikuli. 224pp. 8⅜ × 11¼. 25950-1 Pa. **$9.95**

COMPLETE HUNGARIAN RHAPSODIES FOR SOLO PIANO, Franz Liszt. All 19 Rhapsodies reproduced directly from an authoritative Russian edition. All headings, footnotes translated to English. Best one volume edition available. 224pp. 8⅜ × 11¼. 24744-9 Pa. **$11.95**

ANNÉES DE PÈLERINAGE, COMPLETE, Franz Liszt. Authoritative Russian edition of piano masterpieces: *Première Année (Suisse): Deuxième Année (Italie)* and *Venezia e Napoli; Troisième Année,* other related pieces. 288pp. 9⅜ × 12¼. 25627-8 Pa. **$13.95**

COMPLETE ETUDES FOR SOLO PIANO, Series I: Including the Transcendental Etudes, Franz Liszt, edited by Busoni. Also includes Etude in 12 Exercises, 12 Grandes Etudes and Mazeppa. Breitkopf & Härtel edition. 272pp. 8⅜ × 11¼. 25815-7 Pa. **$14.95**

COMPLETE ETUDES FOR SOLO PIANO, Series II: Including the Paganini Etudes and Concert Etudes, Franz Liszt, edited by Busoni. Also includes Morceau de Salon, Ab Irato. Breitkopf & Härtel edition. 192pp. 8⅜ × 11¼. 25816-5 Pa. **$10.95**

SONATA IN B MINOR AND OTHER WORKS FOR PIANO, Franz Liszt. One of Liszt's most performed piano masterpieces, with the six Consolations, ten *Harmonies poetiques et religieuses,* two Ballades and two Legendes. Breitkopf & Härtel edition. 208pp. 8⅜ × 11¼. 26182-4 Pa. **$12.95**

PIANO TRANSCRIPTIONS FROM FRENCH AND ITALIAN OPERAS, Franz Liszt. Virtuoso transformations of themes by Mozart, Verdi, Bellini, other masters, into unforgettable music for piano. Published in association with American Liszt Society. 247pp. 9 × 12. 24273-0 Pa. **$13.95**

MEPHISTO WALTZ AND OTHER WORKS FOR SOLO PIANO, Franz Liszt. Rapsodie Espagnole, Liebestraüme Nos. 1–3, Valse Oubliée No. 1, Nuages Gris, Polonaises Nos. 1 and 2, Grand Galop Chromatique, more. 192pp. 8⅜ × 11¼. 28147-7 Pa. **$13.95**

COMPLETE WORKS FOR PIANOFORTE SOLO, Felix Mendelssohn. Breitkopf and Härtel edition of Capriccio in F# Minor, Sonata in E Major, Fantasy in F# Minor, Three Caprices, Songs without Words, and 20 other works. Total of 416pp. 9⅜ × 12¼. Two-vol. set. 23136-4, 23137-2 Pa. **$23.90**

COMPLETE SONATAS AND VARIATIONS FOR SOLO PIANO, Johannes Brahms. All sonatas, five variations on themes from Schumann, Paganini, Handel, etc. Vienna Gesellschaft der Musikfreunde edition. 178pp. 9 × 12. 22650-6 Pa. **$10.95**

COMPLETE SHORTER WORKS FOR SOLO PIANO, Johannes Brahms. All solo music not in other two volumes. Waltzes, Scherzo in E Flat Minor, Eight Pieces, Rhapsodies, Fantasies, Intermezzi, etc. Vienna Gesellschaft der Musikfreunde. 180pp. 9 × 12. 22651-4 Pa. **$10.95**

COMPLETE TRANSCRIPTIONS, CADENZAS AND EXERCISES FOR SOLO PIANO, Johannes Brahms. Vienna Gesellschaft der Musikfreunde edition, vol. 15. Studies after Chopin, Weber, Bach; gigues, sarabandes; 10 Hungarian dances, etc. 178pp. 9 × 12. 22652-2 Pa. **$12.95**

PIANO MUSIC OF ROBERT SCHUMANN, Series I, edited by Clara Schumann. Major compositions from the period 1830–39; *Papillons,* Toccata, Grosse Sonate No. 1, *Phantasiestücke, Arabeske, Blumenstück,* and nine other works. Reprinted from Breitkopf & Härtel edition. 274pp. 9⅜ × 12¼. 21459-1 Pa. **$14.95**

PIANO MUSIC OF ROBERT SCHUMANN, Series II, edited by Clara Schumann. Major compositions from period 1838–53; *Humoreske, Novelletten,* Sonate No. 2, 43 *Clavierstücke für die Jugend,* and six other works. Reprinted from Breitkopf & Härtel edition. 272pp. 9⅜ × 12¼. 21461-3 Pa. **$13.95**

PIANO MUSIC OF ROBERT SCHUMANN, Series III, edited by Clara Schumann. All solo music not in other two volumes, including *Symphonic Etudes, Phantaisie,* 13 other choice works. Definitive Breitkopf & Härtel edition. 224pp. 9⅜ × 12¼. 23906-3 Pa. **$11.95**

PIANO MUSIC 1888–1905, Claude Debussy. Deux Arabesques, Suite Bergamesque, Masques, first series of Images, etc. Nine others, in corrected editions. 175pp. 9⅜ × 12¼. 22771-5 Pa. **$8.95**

COMPLETE PRELUDES, Books 1 and 2, Claude Debussy. 24 evocative works that reveal the essence of Debussy's genius for musical imagery, among them many of the composer's most famous piano compositions. Glossary of French terms. 128pp. 8⅜ × 11¼. 25970-6 Pa. **$7.95**

PRELUDES, BOOK I: The Autograph Score, Claude Debussy. Superb facsimile reproduced directly from priceless autograph score in Pierpont Morgan Library in New York. New Introduction by Roy Howat. 48pp. 8⅛ × 11. 25549-2 Pa. **$8.95**

PIANO MASTERPIECES OF MAURICE RAVEL, Maurice Ravel. Handsome affordable treasury; *Pavane pour une infante defunte, jeux d'eau, Sonatine, Miroirs,* more. 128pp. 9 × 12. (Not available in France or Germany) 25137-3 Pa. **$8.95**

COMPLETE LYRIC PIECES FOR PIANO, Edvard Grieg. All 66 pieces from Grieg's ten sets of little mood pictures for piano, favorites of generations of pianists. 224pp. 9⅜ × 12¼. 26176-X Pa. **$11.95**

*Available from your music dealer or write for **free** Music Catalog to Dover Publications, Inc., Dept. MUBI, 31 East 2nd Street, Mineola, N.Y. 11501.*